The Call to Follow Jesus

KAY ARTHUR

HARVEST HOUSE™ PUBLISHERS

EUGENE, OREGON

Cover design by Koechel Peterson & Associates, Minneapolis, Minnesota

The New Inductive Study Series
THE CALL TO FOLLOW JESUS

Copyright © 1994 by Precept Ministries International
Published by Harvest House Publishers
Eugene, Oregon 97402
www.harvesthousepublishers.com

Library of Congress Cataloging-in-Publication Data

Arthur, Kay, 1933–
      The call to follow Jesus / Kay Arthur.
          p. cm. — (The new inductive study series)
      ISBN-13: 978-0-7369-0797-2
      ISBN-10: 0-7369-0797-1
      1. Bible. N.T. Luke—Study and teaching.   2. Bible. N.T. Luke—Criticism,
   interpretation, etc. I. Title. II. Series: Arthur, Kay, 1933–The new inductive
study series.
      BS2596.A59   1994
      226.4'007—dc20   93-33926
                                                              CIP

Printed in the United States of America.

   07 08 09 10 11 12 13 14 15 / BP-MS / 15 14 13 12 11 10 9 8 7 6

CONTENTS

~~~~~~

How to Get Started... 5

The Cost of Following Jesus 15

Week One
Nothing Is Impossible with God 17

Week Two
Where's the Fruit of Repentance? 23

Week Three
Following Christ—A Matter of
    Obedience, Not Qualification 29

Week Four
The Love of the Forgiven 33

Week Five
No Looking Back 37

Week Six
Stay at His Feet 41

Week Seven
Whom Will We Trust? 45

Week Eight
The Cost of Following Jesus 49

Week Nine
God Knows Our Hearts 53

Week Ten
The Danger of Riches 57

Week Eleven
True Faith Is Seen in Its Works 61

Week Twelve
    The Reward of Faith's Obedience............ 67
Week Thirteen
    Be His Witness 73

How to Get Started...

~~~~~

Sometimes it's hard to read directions. You simply want to get started, and only if all else fails will you read the directions. I understand, but in this case, don't do it! These instructions are part of getting started, and they will help you greatly.

FIRST

As you study the book of Luke, you will need four things in addition to this book:

1. A Bible that you are willing to mark in. The marking is essential. An ideal Bible for this purpose is *The New Inductive Study Bible (NISB)*. The *NISB* is in a single-column text format with larger, easy-to-read type, which is ideal for marking. The margins around the text are wide for note-taking.

The *NISB* also has instructions for studying each book of the Bible, but it does not contain any commentary on the text, nor is it compiled from any theological stance. Its purpose is to teach you how to discern truth for yourself through the inductive method of study. (The various charts and maps that you will find in this study guide are taken from the *NISB*.)

Whatever Bible you use, just know you will need to mark in it, which brings me to the second item you will need...

2. A fine-point, four-color ballpoint pen or various colored fine-point pens that you can use to write in your Bible.

3. Colored pencils or an eight-color Pentel pencil (available at most office supply stores).

4. A composition book or notebook for working on your assignments and recording your insights.

SECOND

Though you will be given specific instructions for each day's study, there are basic things you'll want to look for and do as you study each chapter. Let me list them for you. Read them, but don't be overwhelmed. Eventually, they will become a habit.

1. As you read, note the events or teachings of Jesus covered in each chapter by asking the following questions of the text:

a. **What** are the events and/or teachings?

b. **Why** do they happen?

c. **When** do they occur? Watch for their timing. For instance, certain events or teachings might be provoked for different reasons. The "when" of events or teachings may be expressed in several different ways: by mentioning an actual year, month, day, or by mentioning an event, such as a feast, a year of a person's reign, etc., or by using words such as *then, when, afterwards, at this time,* etc. Mark time phrases by putting a clock (like the one shown here) in the margin next to the verse where they appear or over the word that indicates the time. You may want to underline or color the references to time in one specific color.

d. **Where** do these events or teachings take place?

e. **Why** did God think this was important enough to include in His Word? Ask yourself, "What lessons can I learn from these events or teachings for my own life?"

Every day when you finish your lesson, meditate on what you saw and ask your heavenly Father how you should live in the light of the truths you have just seen. At times, depending on how God has spoken to you, you might even want to record these "Lessons for Life" in the margin of your Bible next to the text you studied. The *NISB* suggests you simply put "LFL" in the margin of your Bible and then as briefly as possible record the lesson for life you want to remember.

2. There are certain key words you will want to mark in a special way throughout the Gospel of Luke. This is the purpose of the colored pencils and the colored pen. Developing the habit of marking your Bible in this way will make a significant difference in the way you study and in how much you remember.

A **key word** is an important word that is used by the author repeatedly in order to convey his message to his reader. There are certain key words that will show up throughout the Gospel of Luke, while others will be concentrated in certain chapters or segments of Luke. The following are key words you will find throughout Luke. You will want to mark them and their pronouns (*he, his, she, her, it, we, they, us, our, you, them, their*) as well as any synonyms in a distinguishable color or way:

> *Son of Man*
>
> *follow Me* (or *disciple,* since a disciple is a follower, *a learner*)

> *kingdom of God*
>
> *covenant*
>
> *demons* (or any reference to *Satan, the devil, evil* or *unclean spirits*)
>
> *parable*
>
> *Pharisees*
>
> *scribes and lawyers*

You need to devise a color-coding system for these words so that when you look at a page of your Bible, you will instantly see where a particular word is used. When you start marking key words in various colors and symbols, it is easy to forget how you are marking certain words. You may wish to use the bottom portion of the perforated card in the back of this book to write the key words on. Mark the words the way you plan to mark them in your Bible and then use the card as a bookmark.

I color the word *covenant* the same way throughout my *NISB*. I color it red and box it in yellow. And references to the devil and his cohorts can easily be seen because I mark these with a red pitchfork ✎ . Marking words for easy identification can be done by colors, symbols, or a combination of colors and symbols. However, colors are easier to distinguish than symbols. If I use symbols, I keep them very simple. For example, I color *repent* yellow but put a red arrow ⟶ over it also. The symbol conveys the meaning of repent: a change of mind.

When I mark the members of the Godhead (which I do not always mark), I color every reference to the Father, Son, or Holy Spirit in yellow. I also use a purple pen and mark the Father with a triangle △ , symbolizing the Trinity. I mark the Son this way ⟶ , and the Holy Spirit this way 〰 .

3. Because locations are important in a historical or biographical book of the Bible, you will also find it helpful to mark these in a distinguishable way. I simply underline every reference to location in green (grass and trees are green!), using my four-color ballpoint pen.

I also look up the locations on maps so I can put myself into context geographically. On page 25 of this book, you will find a map taken from the *NISB* that shows you the geographical locations of Jesus' ministry. Use it until you become familiar with these places—it will mean so much more to you when you study the Bible.

4. When you finish studying a chapter of Luke, record the main theme of that chapter on the LUKE AT A GLANCE chart (located at the end of this study book). Record it under the appropriate chapter number. (If you have an *NISB*, there's an identical chart at the end of Luke.) When you finish this survey course, you will have a permanent record of the content of each chapter of Luke right at your fingertips.

5. If you are doing this study within the framework of a class and you find the lessons too heavy, then simply do what you can. To do a little is better than to do nothing. Don't be an all-or-nothing person when it comes to Bible study.

Remember, any time you get into the Word of God, you enter into more intensive warfare with the devil (our enemy). Why? Every piece of the Christian's armor is related to the Word of God. And our one and only offensive weapon is the sword of the Spirit, which is the Word of God. The enemy wants you to have a dull sword. Don't cooperate! You don't have to!

6. There is a chart by Dr. Irving Jensen on the events covered in Luke and how they fit chronologically within

the other Gospel accounts. Familiarize yourself with this excellent chart, which this godly scholar has given us permission to use. It is found on page 78.

7. Always begin your studies with prayer. As you do your part to handle the Word of God accurately, you must remember that the Bible is a divinely inspired book. The words that you are reading are truth, given to you by God that you might know Him and His ways. These truths are divinely revealed.

> For to us God revealed them through the Spirit;
> for the Spirit searches all things, even the depths
> of God. For who among men knows the thoughts
> of a man except the spirit of the man which is in
> him? Even so the thoughts of God no one knows
> except the Spirit of God (1 Corinthians 2:10,11).

Therefore, ask God to reveal His truth to you, to lead you and guide you into all truth. He will, if you will ask.

THIRD

This study book is designed to put you into the Word of God on a *daily* basis. Since man does not live by bread alone but by every word that comes out of the mouth of God, we each need a daily helping.

The assignments cover seven days; however, the seventh day is different from the other days. On the seventh day, the focus is on a major truth covered in that week's study.

You will find a verse or two to memorize and STORE IN YOUR HEART. Then there is a passage to READ AND DISCUSS. This will be extremely profitable for those who are using this material in a class setting, for it will cause the class to focus their attention on a critical portion of

Scripture. To aid the individual and/or the class, there's a set of QUESTIONS FOR DISCUSSION OR INDIVIDUAL STUDY. This is followed with a THOUGHT FOR THE WEEK which will help you understand how to walk in the light of what you learned.

When you discuss the week's lesson, be sure to support your answers and insights from the Bible itself. Then you will be handling the Word of God in a way that will find His approval. Always examine your insights by carefully observing the text to see what it *says*. Then, before you decide what a Scripture or passage *means*, make sure you interpret it in the light of its context.

Scripture will never contradict Scripture. If it ever seems to, you can be certain that somewhere something is being taken out of context. If you come to a passage that is difficult to deal with, reserve your interpretations for a time when you can study the passage in greater depth.

Books in The New Inductive Study Series are survey courses. If you want to do a more in-depth study of a particular book of the Bible, we would suggest you do a Precept Upon Precept Bible Study Course on that book. You may obtain more information on these studies by contacting Precept Ministries at 800-763-8280, visiting our website at www.precept.org, or by filling out and mailing the response card in this book.

LUKE

THE COST OF
FOLLOWING JESUS...

∾∾∾∾∾

Jesus made it very clear: If you want to be His disciple, then you must deny yourself, take up your cross, and follow Him.

He made it clear, and in doing so, to use the proverbial statement taken from a tennis game, *He put the ball in our court.*

What will we do with it? Granted, it is a high-powered ball—a difficult serve, but not impossible to return. Will we let it go by, not return it, and lose what we could have won—the highest of all callings? What fools we would be! What profit would it be to gain anything else, even the whole world, and lose our lives and their purpose?

What about the cost? The cost is high. Jesus urged us to count it. That's what this survey study of the Gospel of Luke will help you do.

The cost is denying self, which in this day and age, even in Christendom, is not popular teaching. The cost is death to self, when in our times many people are trying to discover self and take care of self. The cost is to follow Jesus as a habit of life for the rest of your life! That's not easy when you are playing it out in the world's court, and the grandstands are filled with a multitude shouting, "Fool! You're a fool! Get off the court!"

Oh, my friend, if you are going to deny yourself, take up your cross, and follow Jesus, you had better know with certainty whom you are following, what He is like, what He believes, how He lived in this adverse world, and why and

15

how He died. You also better "know that you know" whether His death was the end of it all or only the beginning.

Discovering all this is the purpose of your study of the Gospel of Luke. Although this is a survey course, as you get information you will become awed at your familiarity with the content of this Gospel and of the inductive study methods that will become habits by the repeated doing of them.

Whether you do this study on your own or with others, I promise you it will be a profitable 13 weeks. However, it will only be as profitable as the discipline you put into it—enough discipline to truly see and understand what it means to be a disciple.

Then, having come face-to-face with the claims and call of Jesus Christ, you can make a rational, sane decision about denying self, taking up your cross, and following Jesus. Your decision, one way or the other, will change the course of your life and consequently have eternal ramifications.

NOTHING IS IMPOSSIBLE WITH GOD

DAY ONE

Simply read through Luke 1, the whole chapter, to put you into context. As you read, note to whom this Gospel was written and why it was written. When you discover this information, you will also know how Luke lays out his material. When you find the verses that give you this information, you might want to write the following in the margin of your Bible: *Purpose for writing*.

DAY TWO

As you saw yesterday, Luke lays out his material in consecutive order: chronologically. It is the only Gospel which does this fully, and therefore it is very valuable to us because it gives us a chronological timeline of the events of Jesus' life from birth through death. Therefore the timing of all the events recorded in the other Gospels can be determined by Luke.

Read through Luke 1 again today.

a) Watch for the various events covered in this chapter. Jot them down in your notebook.

b) Watch for any references to time, such as verse 5: "in the days of Herod, king of Judea." *Underline or color these references to time in a specific color that you can use all the way through your study of Luke.* Then every time you see this color (blue, for example), you will know that it is a reference to time. Or you might want to draw a little clock in the margin like this:

c) In another color underline every reference to location. For example, the angel Gabriel was sent to Nazareth (verse 26). Underline *Nazareth* in green. If you will mark geographical locations in the same way throughout Luke, you will be able to see where Jesus went and what happened in each place.

DAY THREE

Read Luke 1:5-25. You might want to mark every reference to Zacharias in one distinctive way (or color) and every reference to Elizabeth in another. Mark the personal pronouns that refer to them *(he, she)* in the same way that you mark their name. Then in your notebook list what you learn about *Zacharias* and about *Elizabeth*. What do you learn from their lives? (As you make your lists on different people, be sure to leave space to add to the lists so you can continue to record what you learn as you go through Luke.) Describe the event covered in this passage in as few words as possible. If you wish, write this in the margin of your Bible next to verse 5.

DAY FOUR

Read Luke 1:26-38. In a color or way that is distinctive from Zacharias and Elizabeth, mark every reference to Mary and then every reference to her Son, Jesus, along with the personal pronouns. Then list in your notebook what you learn from marking these references. The list on Jesus will be especially important, for this is the One who will later call us to follow Him. We want to know all we can about the One we might choose to follow.

How would you describe the event covered in these verses? Write it out, and if you wish, record this in your Bible as you did yesterday.

DAY FIVE

Read Luke 1:39-56. Continue to mark the reference to each of the main characters in this chapter, and then add what you learn to the lists that you have begun.

What happens in these verses? Record it in your Bible next to verse 39 if you desire.

DAY SIX

Read Luke 1:57-80. What event is covered in these verses?

As you have been doing, mark each reference to your main characters and add what you learn to the list you are making about them.

If you have time you may want to review Luke 1 and make a list of everything you learn from this chapter about

God the Father and about the Holy Spirit. As you see what you learn about God, give special attention to verses 67 to 79.

Record the theme of Luke 1 on the LUKE AT A GLANCE chart (page 77). The theme of a chapter is discerned by observing the subject or the person which is dealt with the most in that chapter. You may also want to record the theme in your Bible by the chapter number.

DAY SEVEN

Store in your heart: Luke 1:17.

Read and discuss: Luke 1:67-80 and Malachi 3:1, and what each student learned about John and the events surrounding his conception, his birth, and the years previous to his public ministry.

QUESTIONS FOR DISCUSSION OR INDIVIDUAL STUDY

∾ Who wrote the Gospel of Luke and why? What do you learn about the writer? How does this information help you accept this Gospel? How would a familiarity with Luke help you with the other Gospels?

∾ What do you learn from Luke 1 about God and His ways? How does such information affect you?

∾ What did you learn about Jesus from this chapter? If you were to deny yourself, take up your cross, and follow Him, whom would you be following? Is He just another man? Why or why not?

∾ Share one thing you learned from the lives of the different people mentioned in Luke 1 that spoke to your heart personally. What kind of impact did that insight have on your thinking or the way you are going to live?

∾ What does this chapter teach about the virgin birth? Is it important to believe it? Why? You may want to look up the following verses: Isaiah 7:14; 9:6; Romans 5:12; 1 Peter 1:18,19.

THOUGHT FOR THE WEEK

God does what He says He will do—in *His* time and in *His* way. This truth is seen in more than one way in the first chapter of Luke: "Nothing will be impossible with God" (verse 37), or, put in another way, "not any word of God is impossible, void of power." The blessing comes to those who believe: "Blessed is she who believed that there would be a fulfillment of what had been spoken to her by the Lord" (1:45).

May we be like Zacharias, Elizabeth, and Mary: May we believe what God says and may we so know and trust God that we say as Mary said, "Behold, the bondslave of the Lord; may it be done to me according to your word" (1:38).

WHERE'S THE FRUIT OF REPENTANCE?

> *As you read Luke week after week, don't forget to mark the key words you have put on your bookmark.*

DAY ONE

Read through Luke 2 and 3. What is the primary event covered in these chapters? If you have time, read Matthew 2:1-23 and see where this chronologically fits into Luke 2 and 3.

DAY TWO

Read Luke 2:1-20. Mark every reference to time and location as you did in Luke 1. Also note the specific happenings covered in this passage.

As you read any passage it is good to ask the 5 W's and an H: who, what, when, where, why, and how. For instance: Who are the main persons covered in this passage? What is happening? Why is it happening? Where is it happening? How did it happen? What is the end result of it all?

You'll find out that you learn a great deal when you interrogate the text this way.

DAY THREE

Read Luke 2:21-40. What events are covered in this segment? Examine each event in the light of the 5 W's and an H. Mark location and time as you have done previously in chapter 1. Check locations on the map on the next page. What do you learn regarding Simeon and Anna? Make a list.

DAY FOUR

Read Luke 2:21-40 again, then Leviticus 12. Why were Mary, Joseph, and Jesus in Jerusalem? What do you learn about Jesus from observing this chapter? Make a list. If you want to have this list before you and there is room, write it in the margin of your Bible.

DAY FIVE

Read Luke 2:41-52. No other Gospel records the events of these verses. What do you learn from them about Jesus? What kind of example do you see that you could follow?

Record the theme of Luke 2 either in your Bible or on the LUKE AT A GLANCE chart (page 77).

DAY SIX

Read Luke 3. As you have done previously, mark all references to events, time, and locations. Luke is a historical and biographical account of the life of Jesus. If you have an *NISB*, look at the colored chart THE HISTORY OF ISRAEL in the front of the Bible and put yourself into time context, noting the years when Pilate was governor of Judea.

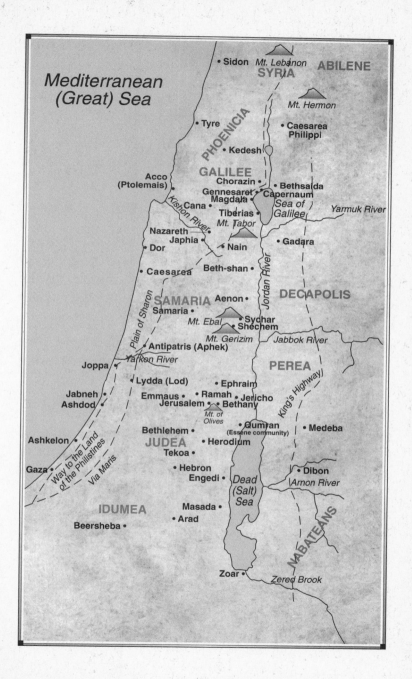

List what you learn about John and about Jesus from this chapter.

DAY SEVEN

Store in your heart: Luke 2:30-32 or 3:16.

Read and discuss: Luke 3:3-18; Matthew 3:4-12; Luke 1:15-17; Malachi 4:6.

QUESTIONS FOR DISCUSSION OR INDIVIDUAL STUDY

∾ What was to be the ministry of John, whom we refer to as "John the Baptist"? There is some stereotypical thinking about John the Baptist—for example, that he ranted and raved, screaming at people to repent. Does this fit what the text says about him?

∾ What was John's message? What was its purpose? How could you tell if his message had an impact—what would those who believed it do?

∾ Did John fulfill his ministry? What did it cost him?

∾ According to John, who was Jesus and what would He do? What did God say about Jesus at His baptism? What does this tell you about the One you might choose to follow?

∾ How old was Jesus when He began His ministry? What do you learn about His example up until that time?

∾ What have you learned this week that you can apply to your own life?

THOUGHT FOR THE WEEK

Luke 3:18 says that John preached the gospel to the people. What do we see John doing? He called people to repentance and reminded them that true repentance can be seen; it bears fruit. What is the fruit or evidence of our repentance?

John pointed people to Jesus, not to himself. He told them what Jesus would do and warned them about the wrath of God. John fulfilled his ministry even though it cost him his freedom.

How well are we doing when it comes to preaching the gospel? Do we give the full story? Are we willing to stand true to the gospel, not watering it down, even though it may cost us our freedom?

FOLLOWING CHRIST— A MATTER OF OBEDIENCE, NOT QUALIFICATION

DAY ONE

Read Luke 4. Note the main events in this chapter— when they occur and where they occur. Mark the references to location and time as you have been doing.

DAY TWO

Read Luke 4:1-13; Matthew 4:1-11; Mark 1:10-13. List everything you observe about Jesus' temptation. Interrogate the whole event with the 5 W's and an H.

DAY THREE

Read Luke 4:14-30. Note carefully the two different locations mentioned in 4:14-16. To appreciate the time-span covered in these verses, look at the chart LIFE OF CHRIST SHOWING COVERAGE BY LUKE (page 78). Note where Luke 4:13 is versus 4:14.

Examine the event covered in 4:16-30 with the 5 W's and an H. Then list what you learn about this One who is later going to call us to deny ourselves, take up our cross, and follow Him.

DAY FOUR

Read Luke 4:31-44. Mark every reference to the demons and their pronouns. You might want to do this with a red pitchfork (it will be easy to spot). You will want to do this all the way through your study of Luke. Keep a list of what you learn from marking every reference to the devil, demons, and unclean spirits. You will learn much that will help you in spiritual warfare. One of the major principles of successful warfare is accurate knowledge of your enemy.

Note also what you learn about Jesus and His ministry from this passage.

DAY FIVE

Read Luke 5:1-16. Mark all references to time and location. Notice what events are covered in these verses. What do you learn about Jesus in this passage? Write down the main things.

Who followed Jesus? Why? What did it cost them?

DAY SIX

Read Luke 5:17-39. List the events covered in this part of chapter 5. Then examine this text event by event. Note what you learn about Jesus from each of these events.

Watch Jesus' critics, what they criticize, and how Jesus handles their criticism.

DAY SEVEN

Store in your heart: Luke 5:16 or 5:31,32.
Read and discuss: Luke 4:18,19; 4:18-32.

QUESTIONS FOR DISCUSSION OR INDIVIDUAL STUDY

∾ According to Luke 4:18,19, what was Jesus' calling?

∾ What do you see in Luke 4 and 5 that will show you how Jesus intended to fulfill His calling? Would He do it alone?

∾ How did the religious leaders in Nazareth and the scribes and the Pharisees respond to God's purpose for Jesus?

∾ If you follow Jesus, do you think you might experience any of the same things? Have you already?

∾ Who all did Jesus call in Luke 4 and 5 to follow Him? What kind of people were they? Answer the 5 W's and an H in respect to their calling.

THOUGHT FOR THE WEEK

If you are excusing yourself from following Jesus, from being His disciple, because of your past or because of your lack of formal training, you need to review Luke 4 and 5 and remember whom Jesus came for and whom Jesus called. Is there any difference between those He came to save and those He called? Of course not! We all came out of the same slave market of sin. Following Jesus Christ is a matter of obedience, not qualification.

For consider your calling, brethren, that there were not many wise according to the flesh, not many mighty, not many noble; but God has chosen the foolish things of the world to shame the wise, and God has chosen the weak things of the world to shame the things which are strong, and the base things of the world and the despised God has chosen, the things that are not, so that He may nullify the things that are, so that no man may boast before God.

But by His doing you are in Christ Jesus, who became to us wisdom from God, and righteousness and sanctification, and redemption, so that, just as it is written, "LET HIM WHO BOASTS, BOAST IN THE LORD" (1 Corinthians 1:26-31).

THE LOVE
OF THE FORGIVEN

DAY ONE

Read Luke 6. Note the main events covered in this chapter, their location, and any indication of when they occur.

DAY TWO

Read Luke 6:1-19; Exodus 20:8-11; 31:12-18; Leviticus 23:3. According to the Law as laid out in the Old Testament books of the Law, had Jesus violated the Sabbath? Would Jesus violate the Law? Read Matthew 5:17-19.

DAY THREE

Read Luke 6:20-49. Mark each occurrence of the following words in a way that will help you see their repetition but distinguish them one from another: *blessed, woe.*

DAY FOUR

Read Luke 6:20-49. Look for Jesus' specific instructions. Either number them in the text as shown in the example that follows:

But I say to you who hear, 1 love your enemies, 2 do good to those who hate you, 3 bless those who curse you, 4 pray for those who mistreat you (Luke 6:27,28).

or list the instructions in your notebook.

DAY FIVE

Read Luke 7:1-35. Once again note the main events covered in this chapter, when they occur, and where they occur. Look up these locations on the map on page 25.

Mark any reference to the devil, demons, or unclean spirits as you did before. Note what you learn from marking these.

Mark every reference to John the Baptist and then make a list of all you learn about him.

What do you learn about Jesus from these verses?

DAY SIX

Read Luke 7:36-50. Mark every reference to the woman in a distinctive way. List everything you learn about her, including how Jesus deals with her.

Make sure you look for lessons that you can apply to your own life, and to your relationship to others, if you are going to be a true follower of Jesus Christ.

DAY SEVEN

Store in your heart: Luke 7:47 or 7:50.
Read and discuss: Luke 6:20-49.

QUESTIONS FOR DISCUSSION OR INDIVIDUAL STUDY

∾ If we are going to follow Jesus, what should be our response to Luke 6:20-49? What would it take to live such a life? What is Jesus calling us to?

∾ Who are blessed and why? Who suffer woe and why?

∾ According to this passage, what does it really mean to call Jesus Lord?

∾ What does our fruit show? What do you think fruit is? How is fruit manifested?

∾ What did you learn about Jesus Christ this week? Whom did He encounter and how did He treat them?

∾ How did He handle John the Baptist when John began questioning whether Jesus was truly the Messiah? What does this teach you about Jesus? About handling people who are dealing with doubt?

∾ What was the most significant truth you saw this week? How did it impact you and why?

THOUGHT FOR THE WEEK

If we stop and think about it, and are honest, when we look at our lives and relationships in comparison to Jesus' life and relationships, we all have been forgiven much. To stop and think about this will cause us to love Him more, for we will see just how much He forgives us.

Even in our doubting, Jesus doesn't discount us or throw us away as worthless. He knows the pressures we endure when we serve as His messengers, and He gently reminds us who it is we are following. He tells us not to stumble over Him, but to stand in faith.

NO LOOKING BACK

DAY ONE

Read Luke 8:1-21. Mark references to time and location. Also mark any references to the enemy as you have done in the past, and mark every occurrence of the word *believe.*

Give special attention to the parable that Jesus tells, and how it relates to the Word of God. Also note whom Jesus considers His mother and brothers. Do you see any relationship to this and to the parable? What is the soil of your heart like? How do you know?

DAY TWO

Read Luke 8:22-39. Mark the word *faith* the same way you marked *believe* in verses 1-21. Watch the progression of events and where they occur. Note why Jesus rebukes the disciples. Was this fair? Why?

Mark every reference to *demon(s)* and list all you learn about demons from this passage.

DAY THREE

Read Luke 8:40-56. Carefully observe each event. Mark every occurrence of the words *faith* and *believe* (and their synonyms) in the same way. Mark any reference to time or location. Then examine each event in the light of the 5 W's and an H. List the events of chapter 8 in the margin of your Bible next to the verse where each event begins.

DAY FOUR

Read Luke 9:1-17. Note the events of this section and mark all the references to time and location. Look up any unfamiliar places on the map on page 25. Examine each event in the light of the 5 W's and an H.

DAY FIVE

Read Luke 9:18-36. List everything you learn about Jesus Christ from this passage.

According to this passage, what does it take to be followers of Jesus Christ? Examine this in the light of the 5 W's and an H. List everything you learn from this text.

DAY SIX

Read Luke 9:37-62, concentrating on one event at a time. Mark references to time, location, and demons, and in a distinctive way mark every occurrence of the word *follow*. Then list those who wanted to or were called to follow Jesus. Note what was said to each and/or how each responded to Jesus' call to follow Him.

DAY SEVEN

Store in your heart: Luke 9:23,24.
Read and discuss: Luke 9:23-27,57-62.

QUESTIONS FOR DISCUSSION OR INDIVIDUAL STUDY

∾ What did you learn from Luke 9 about following the Lord Jesus Christ? Be as thorough in your answer as possible. Discuss to whom this call was given, when it was given, and what the consequences were of not heeding it, if any.

∾ What are some of the excuses that people give for not following Jesus? Why do you suppose God put Luke 9:57-62 in the Bible?

∾ What was the point of the three illustrations in the parable of the sower in Luke 8? What did you learn from the parable about the different responses to the Word of God?

∾ What additional insight does Mark 4:13-20 give us into the various kinds of soil?

∾ Which soil produces fruit? How much? What does the size of the harvest depend on?

∾ What is God's message to us in all this? If you had a soil problem, which soil would you tend to be most like? What can you do to prevent having that kind of soil?

THOUGHT FOR THE WEEK

When God calls us to follow Him, it is to be wherever He says no matter the cost. After all, Jesus is the Christ, the promised Messiah, the Son of God, His chosen One. How we need to listen to and follow Him! Our allegiance is to be to Him above all others, even those most dear to us.

When His call to follow comes, we need to remember that the call is for *now*—not the future. *Now*—and no looking back. What you leave behind will not be worthy to be compared to what you gain.

STAY AT HIS FEET

DAY ONE

Read Luke 10:1-16. As previously, mark all references to time and location. Note the event covered in this passage and examine it in the light of the 5 W's and an H.

DAY TWO

Read Luke 10:17-24. Mark every reference to the devil. Watch what Jesus says the seventy were given and what they were to rejoice about. Why do you think Jesus says this? It is a good question to ponder.

DAY THREE

Read Luke 10:25-37. Note the parable and what prompted the parable. If you want to have a proper understanding of parables, you need to carefully observe the reason Jesus tells a parable. Watch for that single point He wants to drive home and how He does it.

If you have an *NISB*, there is a section at the back of the Bible that explains "Figures of Speech" (pages 2103 to

2106). It covers the subject of parables quite comprehensively. You may want to read it.

DAY FOUR

Read Luke 10:38-42. List everything you learn about Mary and everything you learn about Martha. What lessons can you learn for your own life?

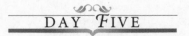

DAY FIVE

Read Luke 11:1-13. List everything you learn about prayer from this passage.

The verbs *ask, seek,* and *knock* are all in the present tense in the Greek, which indicates continued or repeated action. There is a detailed explanation of the various tenses, moods, and voices of Greek verbs in the appendix of the *NISB,* along with a chart that gives you quick information on these (pages 2107 to 2112).

DAY SIX

Read Luke 11:14-36. Note the different situations and/or audiences that Jesus encounters and how He handles each of them. Mark every reference to *Satan* and *demons* (also mark *Beelzebul*) and list what you learn. Observe the text carefully. Don't read anything into it. How does the generation referred to in this passage compare to ours?

DAY SEVEN

Store in your heart: Luke 11:28 or 10:41,42.
Read and discuss: Luke 10:41,42.

QUESTIONS FOR DISCUSSION OR INDIVIDUAL STUDY

∾ What did you learn about Mary and Martha from this account?

∾ The word *distracted* means "to draw from around." What drew Martha away from the Lord?

∾ How would you describe Martha from observing this passage?

∾ According to this passage, what is the one thing that is really needful? How do you get it? How long can you keep it?

∾ Which one of these women do you relate to, and why? (If you have gotten this far in this study, you surely can answer "Mary!" I want you to know you will never be sorry. What you are learning no one will ever be able to take away from you. His Word is different from any other; the words of Jesus are spirit and life [John 6:63]. Press on, valiant one.)

∾ How does a disciple relate to the Word of God? What have you seen in Luke that might help you answer this question? Read John 8:31,32 and discuss it. What do you think it means to abide in His Word?

∾ What did you learn about prayer in your study of Luke 11:1-13?

ভ What relationship do you think there is between prayer
and the Word of God? What biblical support do you
have for your answer? Read John 15:7,16 and discuss it.

THOUGHT FOR THE WEEK

We are to continue to sit at Jesus' feet and learn of Him.
It is to be our lifelong priority and occupation. It is the one
thing that is needful. Everything that makes us what we
ought to be, everything that enables us to do what we do,
even every prayer we pray has its basis in our relationship
to our God and Savior: knowing who He is, what He has
promised, and how we are to live.

We are to persist in that pursuit, and we are to persist
in prayer, as Luke 11:8 teaches. O Beloved, may we ever be
persistent in our pursuit of God and in prayer, for if we are,
we will not fail. And who will enable us to be persistent? Is
it not the blessed Holy Spirit, who is given to everyone who
believes on the Lord Jesus Christ!

WHOM WILL WE TRUST?

DAY ONE

Read Luke 11:37-54. Mark every occurrence of the word *Pharisee* and all pronouns, and then list everything you learn about the Pharisees. A Pharisee was a member of a religious group which provided leadership to the people. They were strict adherents to the Mosaic law.

Also mark every occurrence of the word *lawyers* and its pronouns, and list what you learn about the lawyers. A lawyer, also referred to as a scribe, was an expert in the Mosaic law.

DAY TWO

Read Luke 12:1-12. Note to whom Jesus is speaking in this passage. Mark the words *fear* and *afraid* in the same way. Also mark any reference to the Holy Spirit, as well as the word *beware*. Note what you learn from marking these words.

So many people are tormented by the enemy with the thought that they have blasphemed the Holy Spirit. If you have the time, you might want to look up Matthew 12:22-33 and Mark 3:22-30 to see for yourself what the text says. Do not read anything into it; merely let the Word of God speak for itself.

DAY THREE

Read Luke 12:13-21. Note the setting of this passage and what prompts Jesus to tell the parable He does. Mark the words *possessions (goods)* and *treasure for himself* in the same way. Note what we are to beware of and why.

DAY FOUR

Read Luke 12:22-34. Once again mark the words *possessions* and any synonyms. Also mark any reference to fear and to being anxious as you marked *fear* and *afraid* before.

Now read Luke 12:13-21. Do you see any relationship between these two passages? What? In 12:22, when Jesus says, "For this reason I say to you..." what is the reason?

What is the answer to greed? How does one keep from it? How are you doing? Look up Colossians 3:5 and note what you learn about greed. You might want to write this cross-reference in the margin of your Bible next to Luke 12:15.

DAY FIVE

Read Luke 12:35-48. Mark in the same way every reference to being ready or on the alert. Note why we are to be ready and the consequences of not being ready. Examine this passage very carefully in the light of the 5 W's and an H.

DAY SIX

Read Luke 12:49-59 and 13:1-9. How do these two passages relate to one another? Mark the word *repent*. What do you learn from the passage you are studying today about following Jesus? How can it affect our relationships?

Why do you think Jesus brings up the subject of repentance?

What is the purpose of the parable?

DAY SEVEN

Store in your heart: Luke 12:22,23.
Read and discuss: Luke 12:15-34.

QUESTIONS FOR DISCUSSION OR INDIVIDUAL STUDY

- What is the warning in Luke 12:15-34? How applicable would you say this warning is to the Christian today? Why?

- What did you learn about treasure from this week's study? How did God speak to you about your treasures?

- What is a child of God to seek and why? Is it reasonable to live that way in this day and age?

- What did you learn this week about following Jesus Christ? How could it affect your relationships?

- Why do you think Jesus called the Pharisees hypocrites? Did they really see the condition they were in spiritually?

- Why do you think Jesus told the parable in 13:6-9?

THOUGHT FOR THE WEEK

It is easier to trust in things we can see—to walk by sight rather than faith. It is easier to trust in the arm of the flesh and what we can do ourselves and guarantee ourselves than to put the kingdom of God first and trust God to provide all we need. After all, what if God fails to come through?

God says He knows what we need. Does He really? God says we are to seek His kingdom first and not be anxious about food and clothing because He will provide. But will He?

It all boils down to a matter of faith, doesn't it? Whom will we trust, whom will we believe?

> Thus says the LORD, "Cursed is the man who trusts in mankind and makes flesh his strength, and whose heart turns away from the LORD. For he will be like a bush in the desert and will not see when prosperity comes, but will live in stony wastes in the wilderness, a land of salt without inhabitant.
>
> "Blessed is the man who trusts in the LORD and whose trust is the LORD. For he will be like a tree planted by the water, that extends its roots by a stream and will not fear when the heat comes; but its leaves will be green, and it will not be anxious in a year of drought nor cease to yield fruit" (Jeremiah 17:5-8).

And without faith it is impossible to please Him, for he who comes to God must believe that He is and that He is a rewarder of those who seek Him (Hebrews 11:6).

THE COST
OF FOLLOWING JESUS

DAY ONE

Read Luke 13:10-21. Once again note where Jesus is, what He is doing, and when He is doing it. Watch carefully the response of those present. Remember what you learned about the Sabbath when you looked up the cross-references. Also mark each reference to the enemy, Satan, and his demonic spirits.

You might want to record this event in the margin of your Bible.*

DAY TWO

Read Luke 13:22-30. Note where Jesus is headed and what He is doing as He is going. This is an important passage in respect to salvation, to the future, and to what follows in Luke, so observe it carefully. Watch the question Jesus is asked and how He answers it. Interrogate the passage with the 5 W's and an H.

---

* My prayer is that someday you will make the adjustment to a new Bible and get the *NISB*. The text is easy to read and laid out beautifully. It is easy and spacious to write in, plus there are many other study helps, yet it does not interpret the text for you. Rather, it gives you instructions for studying each book on your own.

Read John 1:11 and Romans 1:16 and think about who heard the good news of the gospel first. What was their general response to the gospel? Meditate on this in the light of what this passage says.

DAY THREE

Read Luke 13:31-35. Note the setting and whom Jesus is dealing with. Remember also what you studied yesterday. What was Jerusalem's house? It was the temple, of course, where the people worshiped God, brought their sacrifices, and celebrated the three annual feasts. Why would their house be left desolate? If you have an *NISB*, look at the colored drawings of the tabernacle and Solomon's temple. Above the Holy of Holies you will see the cloud of God's presence. But look at Herod's temple, which was standing during Jesus' time. There was no cloud of His presence. Was God's presence ever in this temple? Think about Luke 2; what did Simeon see? Jesus, the glory of God, went in and out of that temple during His time on earth. Now what is He saying in Luke 13:34,35? Think about it.

DAY FOUR

Read Luke 14:1-14. Mark the words *eat, feast, reception, luncheon,* or *dinner* all in the same distinctive way. Watch where Jesus is and the occasion for all He is saying. Interrogate the text and note carefully what Jesus is teaching those present.

DAY FIVE

Read Luke 14:15-24. Note how this passage relates to the one preceding it. Continue to mark any reference to a meal as you did yesterday. As you observe this passage, think about those who were first invited. Generally speaking, who were they?

Think about what you studied on Day Two. Then think about what group of people will be invited in. If you have time you would find it profitable to read Ephesians 2:11-22 and 3:4-6.

DAY SIX

Read Luke 14:25-35. Note who is speaking, to whom, and about what—why He is saying what He is saying, etc. Mark the word *disciple* in a distinctive way. A disciple was a learner, a person who followed a certain teacher and adopted his doctrine and his ways. Also mark the word *cost*. Then list what you learn about disciples from this passage and what you learn about the cost. Watch the *therefore*. When you see a *therefore* ask what it is there for.

DAY SEVEN

Store in your heart: Luke 14:26.
Read and discuss: Luke 14:25-35.

QUESTIONS FOR DISCUSSION OR INDIVIDUAL STUDY

- What did you learn from this week's study about being a disciple of Jesus Christ? According to this passage, what would preclude someone from being a disciple of Jesus Christ? Is this fair?

- How does this passage in Luke 14 compare with or add to what you studied in Luke 9:23-27?

∾ Do you see any relationship between Luke 14:25-35 and Luke 14:12-24, since one follows the other? Why weren't the invited people allowed to taste his dinner? What would keep a person from being a disciple?

∾ When you observed Luke 13:22-30, what did you learn about salvation? Can anyone come in any way he or she pleases? Read Matthew 7:13-27 and Luke 6:46-49. Do you see any relationship between these passages?

THOUGHT FOR THE WEEK

From time to time throughout the Gospel of Luke Jesus says, "He who has ears to hear, let him hear." Jesus did not confine Himself to one group or class of people. He didn't isolate Himself and just spend time with His disciples, whether the twelve or the seventy. He ate with publicans and sinners as well as with the scribes and Pharisees. All people had access to Him, and when He spoke to them His explanation of what it meant to follow Him never altered. He laid before them the cost of commitment, the narrowness of the way that led to salvation. Truth cannot be altered and still be truth. Jesus spoke truth—and then called people to hear. The decision to believe and to follow was left up to the hearer.

When we share the gospel, do we make clear exactly what it means to be saved, to be a follower of the Lord Jesus Christ? Do we give a true picture, and do our lives reflect the authenticity of what we teach?

GOD KNOWS OUR HEARTS

DAY ONE

Read Luke 15. As you observe this chapter note what is happening and who is present. Mark the word *parable* and then note what prompts Jesus to tell this parable. When you discover that, write in the margin of your Bible, next to the appropriate verse, "Occasion of the Parable."

DAY TWO

Read Luke 15:1-10. Mark each of the following words in a distinctive way: *lost (loses), found (finds), repents, sinner(s)*.

DAY THREE

Read Luke 15:11-32 and mark the words *sinned, celebrate, rejoice, lost,* and *found.* When you finish, look at the number of stories Jesus told. What do the stories have in common? Stop and think about the key words you marked. Look at *rejoice* and *celebrate.* What brings rejoicing? In any of these stories was there anyone who did not rejoice? Why didn't they? Now think about the occasion or reason Jesus told the parable. What did Jesus want the Pharisees and scribes to see? How did He show them?

DAY FOUR

Read Luke 16:1-13. Mark the word *wealth* and *faithful,* each in a distinctive way. Note to whom Jesus is speaking.

DAY FIVE

Read Luke 16:14-18. Examine this passage carefully, interrogating it with the 5 W's and an H. Note who is there, what they are doing, etc. Ask yourself why Jesus says what He does. Think about all that you have learned about the Pharisees. Did the Pharisees want to enter the kingdom of God? How were they trying to get there? Why does Jesus talk about the Law, and why the mention of adultery? Think on these things.

DAY SIX

Read Luke 16:19-31. After you read through this passage one time, it would probably help you picture it more clearly if you would simply draw it out using stick figures. This account isn't given in any of the other Gospels. What do you learn from it about hades?

Note the context of this story. Is there any correlation to what has preceded it?

DAY SEVEN

Store in your heart: Luke 16:15 or 16:31.
Read and discuss: Luke 16:19-31.

QUESTIONS FOR DISCUSSION OR INDIVIDUAL STUDY

- What did you learn about hades from this passage?

- Why did the rich man want Father Abraham to send someone from the dead to tell his brothers they should repent?

- What was Father Abraham's response?

- Would anyone ever rise from the dead to tell them about the reality of hades? If they wouldn't believe God's Word as recorded in the Old Testament—Moses (the Law) and the Prophets—would they believe the testimony of someone who had died and risen?

- What did you learn from this about the Word of God versus personal testimony?

- How did this account of Lazarus and the rich man fit in with the rest of what you studied this week?

- What have you learned this week?

- What importance or priority do you give to riches and possessions? What place do you think they have in Christendom in our country? What are the lessons we need to learn or remember from our study this week?

THOUGHT FOR THE WEEK

In Luke 16:15 we read that "God knows your hearts." We can justify ourselves in the eyes of other people, but we need to remember that there is One we cannot deceive in any way. He knows us even better than we know ourselves, and this is the One to whom we will someday give an account for the deeds done in our body. This is the only One whom we are to please—the One who searches our hearts, the One who has the full story because He is always there; even the darkness is light to Him.

What is highly esteemed among men is detestable to God (Luke 16:15); therefore let us get our values and priorities in order, according to the Word of God rather than the values of men. Let us look beyond the temporal to the eternal. Let us enter into the kingdom through God's small, narrow gate by listening to His Word and ordering our lives accordingly, for "what does it profit a man to gain the whole world, and forfeit his soul?"(Mark 8:36). Ask the rich man; ask Lazarus.

THE DANGER OF RICHES

DAY ONE

Read Luke 17:1-10 several times. Mark any occurrence of the word *faith*. In verses 1-4, do you see any connection between being a stumbling block, being on your guard, and forgiving? Think about it. Heaven is comprised of what kind of people? What am I saying as a child of God to people I refuse to forgive?

In Luke 17:5-10, what do you learn about faith? Why do you think Jesus says what He does about unworthy slaves or servants? What does He want us to see? What does it have to do with faith—or increasing our faith, which is what the disciples asked Jesus to do?

DAY TWO

Read Luke 17:11-19. Once again mark any reference to *faith*. Also remember to mark references to time and location. What do you learn from this passage that you can apply to your own life?

DAY THREE

Read Luke 17:20-37. As you read this passage, remember to mark the key words on your bookmark. Also mark every use of *day* or *days*. Note whose days they are. Interrogate this passage with the 5 W's and an H. There are some significant things in this passage which are pointing the listeners to a future time when the "Son of Man is revealed" (17:30). Let the text speak for itself without reading into it any of your presuppositions—what you think, what you feel, or what other people have said. You may want to read 2 Thessalonians 1:6-10 in connection with the revelation of the Son of Man on that day.

DAY FOUR

Read Luke 18:1-14. Note the parables that are taught in this passage and why Jesus tells them. What do you learn from these parables that you can apply to your own life?

DAY FIVE

Read Luke 18:15-30. Don't forget to mark words and phrases on your bookmark, especially *the kingdom of God.* Mark the word *follow (-ed, -ing)*. Also mark the words *saved* and *inherit eternal life*—in the same way if you believe the two are synonymous, otherwise in distinctive ways. When you finish, make a list of everything you learn from this passage about the kingdom of God and inheriting eternal life. Ask the 5 W's and an H.

Also note what belongs to those who leave all for the sake of the kingdom of God. Are you willing, Beloved, to leave all if God calls you to?

DAY SIX

. Read Luke 18:31-43. Watch and mark your references to time and location. Note what events are covered in this passage. Note why Jesus and the twelve were going to Jerusalem. You might want to consult the map on page 62 to see how they were going up to Jerusalem. Did what lay before Jesus diminish His concern for others? How do you know from this passage?

DAY SEVEN

Store in your heart: Luke 18:29,30.
Read and discuss: Luke 18:15-30.

QUESTIONS FOR DISCUSSION OR INDIVIDUAL STUDY

∾ What do you learn from this passage about entering the kingdom of God? (It would be good to list these things on a board so you can refer to them in your discussion.)

∾ Discuss what the ruler wanted from Jesus and how Jesus responded. What commands did Jesus leave out when He quoted the commandments? How did Jesus feel about this man? What did Jesus tell the ruler to do? Was the issue salvation? How do you know?

∾ Was Jesus offering the ruler a salvation by works or by faith? Give the reason for your answer.

ᗑ Peter mentioned that they had left their homes and followed Jesus. What was Jesus' response? Is there any
connection between Peter's statement and the account
of the ruler? Explain your answer.

ᗑ Did the ruler get what he wanted? Why?

ᗑ Do you see any connection between this passage and
others in Luke that dealt with salvation and/or following Jesus Christ?

THOUGHT FOR THE WEEK

Faith and obedience seem to be synonymous when it
comes to the kingdom of God. If we truly believe, then we
do the things which God commands. And when we do
what He has commanded, we ought to say, "We are unworthy slaves; we have done only that which we ought to have
done" (Luke 17:10). Faith ought to obey. True faith is seen
in its works; that is why Jesus said to the leper who
returned to thank Him, "Your faith has made you well."

May we not get puffed up by all we do for the kingdom
of God. May we not trust in ourselves that we are righteous
while viewing others as sinners. Instead, may we give
thanks to the One who has been merciful to us as sinners
(18:13).

As we wait for the day of the Son of Man, may we pray
at all times and not lose heart, remembering that "there is
no one who has left house or wife or brothers or parents or
children, for the sake of the kingdom of God, who will not
receive many times as much at this time and in the age to
come, eternal life" (18:29,30).

TRUE FAITH IS SEEN IN ITS WORKS

DAY ONE

Read Luke 19:1-28. Mark the key words on your book-mark. Don't forget to note time and location. What event(s) take place in these verses, and where? Where was Jesus going, and why? Remember what you saw in Luke 18:31 and following.

Now focus on Luke 19:1-10. Note all you learn about Zaccheus and what you learn about the Lord from this passage and why He even bothered with Zaccheus.

DAY TWO

Read Luke 19:11-27. Why did Jesus tell this parable? What is the point of the parable? What do we learn from this parable about the coming of the kingdom of God? Whom do you think the nobleman represents? Whom do the citizens that are enemies represent? What do you learn from the slaves in this parable that you can apply to your own life?

DAY THREE

Read Luke 19:28-48. Mark references to time and location. Consult the map of Jerusalem following.

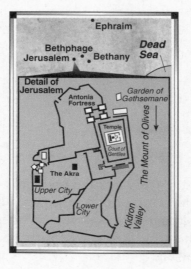

Make a list of the order of events in this chapter. Watch where Jesus is when certain things take place. Note how the multitudes respond and how the Pharisees respond.

DAY FOUR

Read Luke 19:29-40 and Zechariah 9:9. What was happening when Jesus rode into Jerusalem on a donkey? If the people knew the Old Testament Scriptures what could they know? See how important it is to know the Word! (You are to be commended, my friend, for your diligent study and perseverance. Remember, it can never be taken away from you.)

Read Luke 19:41-44 again. Why did Jesus weep (with loud crying)? What did He tell them was coming? Why was it coming?

DAY FIVE

Read Luke 19:45–20:19. Mark the key words, locations, etc. Mark every reference to the *temple*. When you mark the word *parable,* note what the reason is for the parable. As you read this parable, note the parallels you see between the parable and what is happening. Record your insights in your notebook. Also note if Jesus' audience understood the point of the parable and where they fit in.

DAY SIX

Read Luke 20:20-47. Note how Jesus deals with the religious leaders and note His warning to the people. What do you learn about the leaders from this passage? What will happen to these religious leaders? Why? How does this speak to you?

DAY SEVEN

Store in your heart: Luke 19:10.
Read and discuss: Luke 19:10-27; Daniel 7:13,14.

QUESTIONS FOR DISCUSSION OR INDIVIDUAL STUDY

∾ Throughout Luke Jesus is referred to as "the Son of Man." Those Jews who studied the Scriptures would be aware of the messianic prophecy of Daniel 7:13,14.

Have the class look at these verses and then list on the board everything you learn about the Son of Man from verses 13 and 14. Make sure you note everything these verses teach regarding the kingdom.

∞ What do you learn from this parable about the kingdom of God? Ask and answer the 5 W's and an H as a group.

∞ Whom do the following characters in the parable seem to point to: the nobleman, the slaves, the citizens? Discuss what happens to each if you didn't cover that previously.

∞ Is there any lesson in this parable for us as believers? What is it?

∞ If the citizens represent Jews who were rejecting Jesus Christ and His right to rule over them, had they been given ample opportunity to believe? Adequate proof? Was Jesus truly concerned about the "sons of Abraham"? How do you know?

THOUGHT FOR THE WEEK

It is one thing for us to know the Word of God, to be familiar with its content, and to be able to explain what we believe, but all that doesn't do us any good unless we live accordingly.

Jesus wept over Jerusalem because the Jews did not recognize the *time* of their visitation. I wonder how many in the church are like the hypocritical Pharisees who have a religion without a relationship, who can "analyze the appearance of the earth and the sky, but...do...not analyze this present time" (Luke 12:56).

Does Jesus weep over the church?

May we live according to the truth and be good stewards of all that He has given us, for "to everyone who has, more shall be given" (Luke 19:26).

THE REWARD
OF FAITH'S OBEDIENCE

DAY ONE

Read Luke 21 carefully so you get the sense of what is happening and why we are looking at this chapter as a whole. As you read, mark any key words that are on your bookmark for Luke. Mark every reference to the *temple*. Every time you come to the words *before, then,* or *when,* mark them in such a way that you can tell they are indicators of time, giving a sequence of time and events. This is very important.

DAY TWO

Read Luke 21 again. This time note the questions that are asked in verse 7. Write out what the "these things" refer to. Then rephrase the question by substituting what the "these things" refer to.

When you finish doing that, note how Jesus answers the question. Pay careful attention to the time indicators you marked yesterday, for they will help you sort out the sequence of events.

As you read, also mark the words *day(s)* (and any pronouns) and *end,* each in its own distinctive way.

DAY THREE

Read Luke 19:43,44. How does this compare with Luke 21? How does Luke 17:20-30 compare with Luke 21:25-28?

The questions that Jesus answered were "When will the temple be torn down? What will be the sign that the tearing down of the temple is about to take place?"

Jesus answered more than those questions, for He also told His listeners what would happen when they would see "THE SON OF MAN COMING IN A CLOUD with power and great glory" (21:27).

In your notebook, list the events according to Luke 21 that lead up to the destruction of the temple and that follow the destruction of the temple. If you have room you may want to record this list in the margin of Luke 21.

DAY FOUR

Read Luke 22:1-30. Mark key words as well as time and location phrases, and carefully note the sequence of events. If you have an *NISB* you would find it very enlightening to turn to the end of Leviticus and look at the chart THE FEASTS OF ISRAEL (pages 214 and 215).

If you have time, compare Luke 22:28-30 with Luke 14:15-24.

DAY FIVE

Read Luke 22:31-46. Mark your key words. Watch carefully the sequence of events. Look at the diagram of the city of Jerusalem on the next page. As you read all this, remember that these are real people. Jesus is the One who has called you to deny yourself, take up your cross, and follow Him. What is His example? What is He saying to His disciples at this time? What lessons does He have for you in this account, Beloved? Don't miss them.

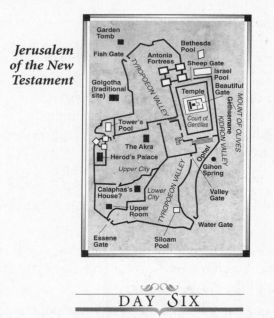

Jerusalem of the New Testament

DAY SIX

Read Luke 22:47-71. Mark your key words, etc. Watch how Jesus interacts with the various people mentioned in this segment of the chapter. Note how Jesus identifies Himself in Luke 22:69 and how they respond. Are they left with any shadow of a doubt about His claim to be Messiah, the Christ?

And what about you? Do you believe He is who He says He is? How then should you live?

DAY SEVEN

Store in your heart: Luke 21:34,35 or 22:69.
Read and discuss: Luke 19:41-44; 21:7-28.

QUESTIONS FOR DISCUSSION OR INDIVIDUAL STUDY

∾ What were the questions the people asked Jesus in Luke 21?

∾ What are the events that precede the destruction of the temple? (If there is any debate at all, simply follow the time indicators that the class members marked and let the text say what it says.)

∾ What events follow the destruction of the temple?

∾ Compare Luke 21:27 with Daniel 7:13. What do you see?

∾ How does all this compare with what you have learned about the kingdom of God as you have marked it throughout the Gospel of Luke?

∾ According to Luke 22:69, where would Jesus go after His crucifixion? Compare this with Mark 14:62 and then look at Luke 21:27. Look at Hebrews 1:13 (a quote from Psalm 110:1) and Hebrews 7:25. Taking all this information and putting it together, what will Jesus do until He comes in a cloud with power and great glory?

∾ What is "the end" as referred to in Luke 21:9?

∾ What is Jesus' word of exhortation at the end of Luke 21? Does it apply to us? Why? How?

THOUGHT FOR THE WEEK

If the Lord were to come today, how do you think He would evaluate the way you are living? Is your heart weighed down with the worries of this life? Are your days dissipated—wasted because you live for your own pleasure and desires rather than for His?

If He were to come today, would you be absolutely shocked because you haven't lived in the anticipation of His coming? What would you change about the way you live, the way you spend your time, the way you spend your money, if you knew that Jesus Christ was coming soon?

May I commend you for studying the Word of God? In Luke 21:8, we see Jesus' warning, "See to it that you are not misled." If you will learn the Word of God—the whole counsel of His Word—and diligently study it, then you won't find yourself easily misled.

Press on, as His valiant warrior.

BE HIS WITNESS

DAY ONE

Read Luke 23:1-25. Mark the key words and watch the sequence of events. Ask the 5 W's and an H about the characters and the events.

DAY TWO

Read Luke 23:26-43. As you read, picture it all in your mind's eye. Imagine what it would be like to be in Jesus' place. Here He is laying down His life for the sins of the whole world, and look at how He is being treated. Watch how He responds. This is the One who is calling you to follow Him. Read Philippians 2:5-11.

Notice what Jesus says to the "daughters of Jerusalem." How does this line up with what you have studied in Luke regarding what is yet to happen in Jerusalem?

DAY THREE

Read Luke 23:44-49. If you have time you would find it enlightening to read Psalm 22, for it gives you greater

73

insight into death by crucifixion. As you study all this, ask God to use it to show you how very much He loves you. "If God is for us, who is against us? He who did not spare His own Son, but delivered Him over for us all, how will He not also with Him freely give us all things? Who will bring a charge against God's elect? God is the one who justifies; who is the one who condemns? Christ Jesus is He who died, yes, rather who was raised, who is at the right hand of God, who also intercedes for us" (Romans 8:31-34).

DAY FOUR

Read Luke 23:50-24:12. Watch the sequence of events and the characters very carefully. If you have time you might want to read the other Gospel accounts to get the complete story of the events surrounding Jesus' resurrection. These can be found in Matthew 27:57-28:15; Mark 15:42-16:14; John 19:38-20:29.

Make a simple chart with four columns (one for each Gospel), and list the events of the resurrection as presented in each Gospel. When you complete your chart, you'll have a thorough account of the event.

DAY FIVE

Read Luke 24:13-43. Mark every reference to the Scriptures in a distinctive way. As you observe this segment of Luke 24, watch carefully for any time phrases or indicators. Notice where the events of Luke 24 occur and their relationship to the death and resurrection of Jesus.

DAY SIX

Read Luke 24:44-53. Mark every reference to the Scriptures as you did yesterday. List what you learn about the Word of God (the Scriptures) from reading yesterday's and today's passages.

Note what is to be proclaimed, where, when, and by whom.

The disciples were to wait for the promise of the Father. Remember what you learned at the beginning of your study, when you looked at the message of John the Baptist? Read Luke 3:16 and Acts 1:1-5.

Acts ought to be the next New Testament study you do, so you get "the rest of the story." After all, who wrote Acts and why? If you didn't notice that, read Acts 1:1-5 again.

DAY SEVEN

Store in your heart: Luke 24:44,45 or 24:25,27.
Read and discuss: Luke 24:38-49.

QUESTIONS FOR DISCUSSION OR INDIVIDUAL STUDY

∞ What was the most piercing or captivating thing you read about the crucifixion of Jesus Christ?

∞ Why is the resurrection so important to Christianity? You might want to read 1 Corinthians 15:12-19 and discuss it.

∞ What is the evidence of the resurrection? Is it substantial evidence? You might want to read 1 Corinthians 15:1-8.

∾ Should Jesus' death or His resurrection have been a surprise?

∾ What were the followers of Jesus to proclaim to the nations? What happened to Jesus that assures that our sins are forgiven? Look at Romans 4:25.

∾ How has God spoken to you through this study of Luke? What are some specific things He has done?

∾ Has it been a struggle to do your assignments, to finish your study? How did you handle it?

∾ What have you learned specifically about being a follower—a disciple—of Jesus Christ?

THOUGHT FOR THE WEEK

Disciples continue in the Word of God; they have to, for it is the very bread by which they live. It is the Word of God that sustains the life of Christ in us, bringing our love for Him to a white-hot heat so that we are not lukewarm.

If Moses, the Psalms, and the Prophets all speak of Jesus, then how important it is that we study the Old Testament as well as the New! As we study, may we never forget that it is Jesus who must open our minds to understand the Scriptures.

Press on, beloved and diligent student. These are critical days. The people who know their God will be strong and take action (Daniel 11:32).

LUKE AT A GLANCE

Theme of Luke:

SEGMENT DIVISIONS

			CHAPTER THEMES
		1	
		2	
		3	
		4	
		5	
		6	
		7	
		8	
		9	
		10	
		11	
		12	
		13	
		14	
		15	
		16	
		17	
		18	
		19	
		20	
		21	
		22	
		23	
		24	

Author:

Date:

Purpose:

Key Words:

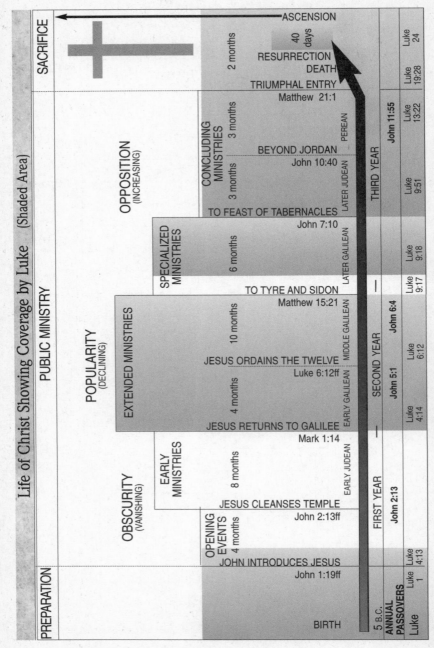

Life of Christ Showing Coverage by Luke (Shaded Area)

PREPARATION	PUBLIC MINISTRY			SACRIFICE

PREPARATION

BIRTH

5 B.C.
ANNUAL PASSOVERS
Luke 1 | Luke 4:13

JOHN INTRODUCES JESUS
John 1:19ff

OBSCURITY (VANISHING)

OPENING EVENTS
4 months

JESUS CLEANSES TEMPLE
John 2:13ff

EARLY MINISTRIES
8 months

FIRST YEAR
John 2:13
EARLY JUDEAN

POPULARITY (DECLINING)

JESUS RETURNS TO GALILEE
Mark 1:14

EXTENDED MINISTRIES
4 months
10 months

JESUS ORDAINS THE TWELVE
Luke 6:12ff

Luke 4:14 | Luke 6:12
EARLY GALILEAN | MIDDLE GALILEAN

SECOND YEAR
John 5:1 | John 6:4

TO TYRE AND SIDON
Matthew 15:21

SPECIALIZED MINISTRIES
6 months

Luke 9:17 | Luke 9:18
LATER GALILEAN

OPPOSITION (INCREASING)

TO FEAST OF TABERNACLES
John 7:10

CONCLUDING MINISTRIES
3 months
3 months
3 months
2 months

BEYOND JORDAN
John 10:40

LATER JUDEAN | PEREAN

TRIUMPHAL ENTRY
Matthew 21:1

DEATH
RESURRECTION
40 days

ASCENSION

Luke 9:51 | Luke 13:22 | Luke 19:28 | Luke 24
John 11:55

THIRD YEAR

Used by permission. Jensen, Irving L. *Luke: A Self-Study Guide.* Chicago: Moody Press, 1970.

NOTES

1. KJV: *devil(s)*
2. NIV: sometimes *not one of us* (for *does not follow us*)
3. KJV: *devils*
4. KJV, NIV, NKJV: *beelzebub*
5. KJV: *cumbered*
6. NIV: *experts in the law*
7. NIV: *be on...guard*
8. NIV: sometimes *good things*
9. NIV: *things for himself*
10. KJV: *that ye have*
    NKJV: *what you have*
11. ESV: *dine*
12. KJV: *wedding (w/o feast)*
    NIV: *banquet*
13. ESV: *banquet*
    KJV, NKJV: *supper*
14. KJV, NKJV: *likewise*
    NIV: *same way*
15. KJV, NKJV: *be (make) merry*
16. ESV, NIV: *be glad*
    KJV, NKJV: *make merry*
17. KJV, NKJV: *mammon*
    ESV, NIV: sometimes *money*
18. NIV: *trusted, trustworthy*
19. NIV: sometimes *time*
20. NIV: sometimes *at that time*
21. NIV: sometimes *time*

Books in the
New Inductive Study Series

❧ ❧ ❧ ❧

Teach Me Your Ways
Genesis, Exodus,
Leviticus, Numbers, Deuteronomy

*Choosing Victory,
Overcoming Defeat*
Joshua, Judges, Ruth

Desiring God's Own Heart
1 & 2 Samuel, 1 Chronicles

Walking Faithfully with God
1 & 2 Kings, 2 Chronicles

*Overcoming Fear
and Discouragement*
Ezra, Nehemiah, Esther

*Trusting God
in Times of Adversity*
Job

*God's Answers for
Today's Problems*
Proverbs

*God's Blueprint
for Bible Prophecy*
Daniel

*Discovering the God
of Second Chances*
Jonah, Joel, Amos, Obadiah

*Finding Hope
When Life Seems Dark*
Hosea, Micah, Nahum,
Habakkuk, Zephaniah

*Opening the Windows
of Blessings*
Haggai, Zechariah, Malachi

The Call to Follow Jesus
Luke

*The God who Cares
and Knows You*
John

*The Holy Spirit
Unleashed in You*
Acts

*God's Answers for
Relationships and Passions*
1 & 2 Corinthians

*Free from Bondage
God's Way*
Galatians, Ephesians

That I May Know Him
Philippians, Colossians

*Standing Firm in
These Last Days*
1 & 2 Thessalonians

*Walking in Power,
Love, and Discipline*
1 & 2 Timothy, Titus

*Living with Discernment
in the End Times*
1 & 2 Peter, Jude

God's Love Alive in You
1, 2, & 3 John,
Philemon, James

Behold, Jesus Is Coming!
Revelation